ALBANIA
TRAVEL GUIDE 2024
(Europe's Last Secret)

Explore all you need to know and Discover the Best Map, Attractions, Itinerary, Beaches, Foods, Festivals and Nightlife on your Trip to Albania.

JOHN P WADE

Disclaimer

All rights reserved. No part of this publication may be reproduced, distributed or transmitted in any form or by any means, including photocopying, recording, or order electronic or mechanical methods without the prior written permission of the publisher, except in the case of brief quotations embodies in critical reviews and certain other noncommercial uses permitted by copyright law.

Copyright © 2023, John P. Wade

ABOUT THE AUTHOR

John P. Wade is a travel guide writer originally from the United States. He has traveled extensively and lived in several countries, which has given him great insight into different cultures and ways of life. His books are known for their thorough research and detailed descriptions of the destinations he visits, and his books are considered the best in the genre.

He is committed to promoting travel and tourism, serves on several industry boards and committees, and is a strong advocate for responsible travel. In his spare time, John enjoys reading, making music, and making some jokes.

Travel is an essential part of life, he believes, and he tries to make his books a reliable source of information and inspiration. He lives in North America with his wife and children and is currently working on his next book.

Be sure to follow him to keep up with his newly published books. You can ask him direct inquiries and questions about this: apehchybest@gmail.com

TABLE OF CONTENT

INTRODUCTION	6
CHAPTER ONE	13
Maps and Directions	13
CHAPTER TWO	37
Planning The Trip	37
CHAPTER THREE	79
Seven (7) Days Itinerary Plan	79
CHAPTER FOUR	90
Top Attractions To Visit In Albania	90
CHAPTER FIVE	120
Beaches In Albania	120
CHAPTER SIX	146

Albania Delicacy	146
CHAPTER SEVEN	174
Nightlife In Albania	174
CHAPTER EIGHT	185
Albania Festivals	185
CHAPTER NINE	205
Safety Tips for Travelling to Albania	205
CONCLUSION	219

INTRODUCTION

Welcome to the alluring country of Albania, a place that captivates visitors with its gorgeous scenery, fascinating history, and vibrant culture. Our thorough guide, "Albania Travel Guide 2024," is your passport to discovering this hidden gem of Europe, which is tucked away in the center of the Balkan Peninsula.

Albania Flag

Albania Capital City: Tirana

Map and Direction

In order to help you understand this complex and intriguing country, our adventure begins with exploring Albania's topography. You'll discover thorough maps and crucial directions within to make sure you never get lost. Our guide will be your dependable travel companion whether you're exploring the historic alleyways of Gjirokastr, strolling through the busy squares of Tirana, or looking for peace along the Albanian Riviera.

Planning the Trip of a Lifetime

Planning a trip to Albania can be a thrilling adventure in itself, and we've got you covered. From visa requirements and transportation options to the best time to visit, "Albania Travel Guide 2024" lays out all the practical information you need to plan your journey seamlessly. We'll help you select the perfect accommodation to suit your style and budget, ensuring a comfortable and memorable stay in Albania.

Seven Days, Seven Adventures: Itinerary Planning

For those seeking a week-long adventure in this captivating land, our seven-day itinerary plan offers a meticulously curated selection of experiences. Explore the archaeological wonders of Butrint National Park, soak in the breathtaking views of Lake Ohrid, and stroll through the vibrant streets of Shkodër. Whether you're an outdoor enthusiast, a history buff, or a culture connoisseur, our itinerary promises to make every day an unforgettable adventure.

Top Attractions to Visit

Albania boasts an abundance of captivating attractions, and our guide shines a spotlight on the must-visit sites. From the historic charm of Berat's Old Town, a UNESCO World Heritage site, to the ancient city of Apollonia, where history comes alive, we'll lead you to the places that will leave you awe-inspired.

Beaches That Define Paradise

Discover Albania's pristine coastline along the Ionian Sea and the Adriatic Sea. Our guide showcases the country's most idyllic beaches, where crystal-clear waters meet untouched shores. Dive into the vibrant beach culture, whether you're looking for relaxation, water sports, or beachfront dining.

Delicious Food: A Gastronomic Journey

Albania's cuisine is a reflection of its rich history and diverse culture. "Albania Travel Guide 2024" introduces you to mouthwatering Albanian dishes like baklava, byrek, and tave kosi. You'll also find recommendations for the best local eateries and markets, ensuring that your taste buds embark on a delectable journey of their own.

Nightlife and Entertainment

As the sun sets over the mountains and coastline, Albania comes alive with a vibrant nightlife scene. Whether you're into dancing the night away at trendy clubs in Tirana or sipping cocktails by the beach in Dhermi, our guide reveals the hottest spots to experience Albania's nightlife at its best.

Safety Tips for Traveling

Your safety is our priority. In "Albania Travel Guide 2024," we provide valuable insights into staying safe while exploring this charming country. From essential travel precautions to local customs and etiquette, we'll help you navigate Albania with confidence.

Embark on a journey like no other as you immerse yourself in the hidden treasures of Albania. With "Albania Travel Guide 2024" in your hand, you'll discover a land of natural beauty, cultural richness, and warm hospitality.

CHAPTER ONE

Maps and Directions

One of the essential tools for any traveler embarking on a journey to a new destination is a comprehensive map and clear directions. Albania, with its diverse landscapes, historical sites, and charming towns, offers an adventure like no other. In this section, we will provide you with a detailed guide to navigating Albania's roads, cities, and hidden gems. Let's begin by exploring the geographical layout of this captivating Balkan nation.

Albania Maps and Facts

Geographical Overview

Albania is a country of remarkable geographical diversity, and understanding its layout is crucial for planning your travel adventure effectively. Situated in Southeastern Europe on the Balkan Peninsula, Albania shares borders with Montenegro to the northwest, Kosovo to the northeast, North Macedonia to the east, and Greece to the south. To the west, it boasts a stunning coastline along the Adriatic Sea, while the Ionian Sea graces its southwestern shores.

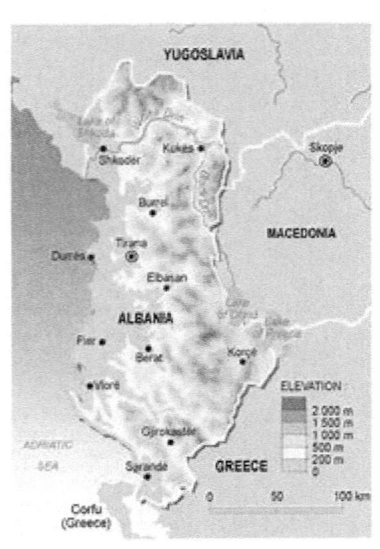

Albania Maps and Facts

Major Regions of Albania

1. The Coastal Region: This region encompasses the entire coastline of Albania along the Ionian Sea and the Adriatic Sea. It is famous for its picturesque beaches, historic towns, and vibrant coastal cities.

2. The Southern Region: Home to the Albanian Riviera, the southern part of the country is known for its pristine beaches, rugged landscapes, and charming villages.

3. The Central Region: This region includes the capital city, Tirana, and is characterized by a mix of modern urban centers, historical sites, and stunning natural parks.

4. The Northern Region: This area is rich in history, with cities like Shkodër and Krujë offering a glimpse into Albania's past. It also boasts breathtaking landscapes and the stunning Lake Shkodër.

5. ***The Eastern Region***: The eastern part of Albania is known for its mountains, national parks, and outdoor recreational opportunities.

6. ***The Southeastern Region***: This region shares a border with Greece and offers a blend of cultural influences, including Greek and Albanian traditions.

Understanding these regions will be instrumental in planning your journey across Albania.

Maps for Your Albanian Adventure

Maps are your trusted companions in exploring Albania's diverse landscapes, picturesque towns, and historical sites. When it comes to maps, here are a few options to consider:

1. Paper Maps: Before embarking on your trip, consider purchasing a physical map of Albania. These are readily available at most bookstores and travel shops. National Geographic and other reputable map publishers often produce detailed maps of Albania, which are ideal for road trips and hiking adventures.

2. *GPS Navigation*: In the digital age, GPS navigation has become an invaluable tool for travelers. Popular GPS navigation apps like Google Maps, Waze, and Maps.me offer detailed maps of Albania, including turn-by-turn directions, points of interest, and real-time traffic updates. Make sure to download the offline maps for Albania to avoid data usage while on the road.

3. *Albanian Road Atlas*: If you plan to explore the country by car extensively, investing in an Albanian road atlas is a wise choice. These atlases provide detailed road maps, information about road conditions, and essential travel tips.

4. *Local Maps*: Once in Albania, you can often find local maps at information centers, hotels, and tourist attractions. These maps are helpful for exploring specific cities or regions in more detail.

Navigating Albanian Roads

Albania's road network has improved significantly in recent years, making it more accessible for travelers. However, there are still some factors to keep in mind when navigating Albanian roads:

1. Road Conditions: While major highways are generally well-maintained, some rural roads may be narrow and winding. Always exercise caution, especially when driving in mountainous areas.

2. Traffic Signs: Pay close attention to traffic signs, which are typically in Albanian. Familiarize yourself with common road signs and their meanings before your trip.

3. Driving Habits: Albanian drivers may have a reputation for their unique driving style. Expect some differences in driving etiquette, such as frequent use of the horn and passing on narrow roads.

4. Speed Limits: Be aware of posted speed limits and adhere to them. Speed limits are enforced by the police, and fines for violations can be hefty.

5. Gas Stations: Fuel stations are plentiful in urban areas but may be less common in remote regions. Always fill up your tank before embarking on long journeys.

Navigating Albania's Cities

Albania's cities, particularly the capital, *Tirana*, can be bustling and chaotic, but they also hold immense charm and cultural treasures. Some tips for navigating Albanian include:

Tirana: Tirana is Albania's biggest city and the nation's political, economic, and cultural hub. While it may seem chaotic at first, you'll quickly adapt to its rhythm. The city offers public transportation options, including buses and taxis.

Public Transportation: Many cities in Albania have public transportation systems, including buses and minibusses. Tirana also has a network of trolleybuses. Familiarize yourself with the routes and schedules if you plan to use public transport.

Taxis: Taxis are readily available in major cities, and they are a convenient way to get around. Make sure to use licensed taxis with meters to avoid overcharging.

Walking: Albanian cities are pedestrian-friendly, and exploring on foot is a great way to soak in the local atmosphere. Many cities have well-preserved historical districts and vibrant marketplaces to explore.

Landmarks: Albanian cities are known for their historical and cultural landmarks. Use your map or navigation app to locate key sites and plan your city exploration accordingly.

Directional Phrases in Albanian

While many Albanians in urban areas understand and speak English, it's always helpful to have a few basic directional phrases in Albanian to assist you during your travels:

- *Drejta (Drey-tah) - Straight*

- *Mbrapa (Em-brah-pah) - Behind*

- *Djathtas (Jat-htahs) - Right*

- *Majtas (My-tahs) - Left*

- *Lart (Lahrt) - Up*

- *Poshtë (Posh-tee) - Down*

- *Afër (Ah-fear) - Near*

- *Larg (Larg) - Far*

- *Në këtë rrugë (Nuh kuhtuh ruh-guh) - On this road*

- *Në rrugën kryesore (Nuh ruh-guhn kry-eh-sor-eh) - On the main road*

Tips for Using Navigation Apps

If you choose to rely on navigation apps during your travels in Albania, do these:

Download Offline Maps: Before your trip, download offline maps for Albania through your preferred navigation app. This ensures you have access to maps and directions even when you don't have a data connection.

Set Your Language: Most navigation apps allow you to select your preferred language for directions. Set it to English or your language of choice for ease of use.

Save Important Locations: Before you leave, save the locations you plan to visit in your navigation app. This way, you can easily navigate to them without typing in addresses every time.

Check for Traffic Updates: Navigation apps often provide real-time traffic updates and alternative routes to avoid congestion. Keep an eye on traffic conditions, especially in urban areas.

Use Voice Navigation: Many apps offer voice-guided navigation, which can be especially helpful while driving. Enable this feature to receive turn-by-turn directions audibly.

Recommended Travel Apps

In addition to navigation apps, several other travel apps can enhance your experience in Albania:

Google Translate: Useful for translating English to Albanian and vice versa, helping you communicate with locals.

XE Currency Converter: Convenient for checking currency exchange rates, which can be essential for budgeting.

Albania Travel Guide Apps: Several apps are dedicated to Albania's attractions, culture, and cuisine, providing valuable insights for travelers.

Weather Apps: Stay informed about weather conditions in different regions of Albania to plan your activities accordingly.

Navigating Albania, with its diverse landscapes and rich cultural heritage, is an adventure filled with excitement and wonder. Whether you're exploring the coastal gems of the Albanian Riviera or the historical sites of ancient cities, having the right maps and directions is crucial for a successful journey. Armed with this knowledge, you are well-prepared to embark on your Albanian adventure in 2024. So, pack your bags, grab your maps, and get ready to explore this hidden gem of the Balkans!

GPS Navigation Technology

In the modern age of travel, GPS navigation technology has revolutionized the way we explore new destinations. Albania is no exception, and travelers can take full advantage of GPS apps and devices to navigate its cities and landscapes.

Popular GPS Navigation Apps include:

Google Maps: Google Maps is one of the most widely used navigation apps worldwide. It offers detailed maps of Albania, turn-by-turn directions, real-time traffic updates, and even public transportation options in some cities. You can also download offline maps to use when you have no internet connectivity.

Waze: Waze is a navigation app with a focus on the community that excels at giving users up-to-the-minute traffic and road information. It's especially useful in urban areas, where it can help you avoid traffic jams and find the quickest routes.

Maps.me: Maps.me is known for its detailed offline maps. Before your trip, download the map of Albania, and you'll have access to navigation even without a data connection. It also offers points of interest, making it easy to find restaurants, hotels, and attractions.

Here WeGo: Here WeGo provides offline maps and navigation with turn-by-turn directions. It's a reliable option for travelers who want to minimize data usage.

Sygic: Sygic is a premium GPS navigation app that offers features like offline maps, real-time traffic information, and speed limit warnings. It's ideal for travelers who prioritize a comprehensive navigation experience.

GPS Devices

For those who prefer dedicated GPS devices, options like Garmin and TomTom are available. Ensure that you purchase a device with pre-loaded maps of Albania or the ability to download them. These devices are especially handy for road trips and outdoor adventures.

Albanian Road Signs and Navigation Phrases

Albania, like many countries, uses its own set of road signs and directional phrases. Familiarizing yourself with these signs and phrases can be immensely helpful while navigating the country's roads.

Common Road Signs in Albania include:

Stop Sign: In Albania, the stop sign is an octagonal red sign with white letters. It's internationally recognized.

Yield Sign: A yield sign in Albania is a white, upside-down triangle with a red border.

Speed Limit Signs: Speed limits in Albania are indicated in kilometers per hour (km/h). Observe the specified speed restrictions and alter your speed as necessary.

One-Way Street: Indicated by a blue circle with a white arrow pointing in the permitted direction.

No Entry: A red circle with a white horizontal bar means you cannot enter the road.

Roundabout: A circular sign with white arrows indicates a roundabout. In a roundabout, you should always yield to oncoming traffic.

Parking Restrictions: Look for signs indicating where you can and cannot park. Blue lines on the side of the road often indicate paid parking areas.

Specialized Maps for Different Types of Travelers

Depending on your interests and travel style, you might want specialized maps to enhance your experience in Albania. These include:

Hiking and Outdoor Adventure Maps

For adventurers seeking to explore Albania's rugged landscapes and national parks, specialized hiking maps can be indispensable. These maps provide topographical details, trail information, and safety tips for outdoor enthusiasts. Popular hiking destinations include the Accursed Mountains and Theth National Park.

Historical and Cultural Maps

Albania is rich in history and culture, and specialized maps highlighting historical sites, museums, and cultural attractions can help you delve deeper into the country's heritage. Maps focusing on UNESCO World Heritage Sites, ancient ruins, and Ottoman-era architecture can make your cultural exploration more immersive.

Culinary and Foodie Maps

Food enthusiasts can seek out specialized maps that pinpoint the best restaurants, street food vendors, and local markets in Albania. Discover the flavors of Albanian cuisine, from traditional dishes like qofte and pite to regional specialties like seafood along the coast.

Beach and Coastal Maps

If your primary goal is to soak up the sun and enjoy the pristine beaches along Albania's coastline, consider using specialized coastal maps. These maps can highlight the most scenic beaches, beachfront resorts, and water sports opportunities.

"Albania Travel Guide 2024" recommends that *Maps and directions are indispensable tools for any traveler exploring Albania in 2024. Whether you choose to rely on GPS navigation apps, paper maps, or specialized maps tailored to your interests, being well-prepared in this regard will enhance your travel experience in this captivating Balkan nation. Armed with the knowledge of navigating Albania's roads, cities, and landscapes, you are ready to embark on an unforgettable journey filled with discovery and adventure. So, let*

your maps be your guide as you explore the hidden treasures of Albania!

CHAPTER TWO

Planning The Trip

Planning Your Albania Trip in 2024

''Albania Travel Guide 2024'' promises an adventure filled with breathtaking landscapes, rich history, and warm hospitality. To ensure that your trip is everything you've dreamed of and more, meticulous planning is key. In this extensive guide, we'll take you through each step of planning your Albania adventure, helping you make the most of this enchanting destination.

When to Visit Albania

The timing of your trip to Albania can greatly influence your experience. Albania experiences distinct seasons, each offering its own unique charm:

Spring (March to May):

Weather: Spring brings mild temperatures, blooming wildflowers, and lush green landscapes.

Advantages: Ideal for outdoor activities like hiking and exploring historical sites without the summer crowds.

Considerations: Be prepared for occasional rain showers.

Summer (June to August):

Weather: Summer is hot and dry, with temperatures often exceeding 30°C (86°F).

Advantages: Perfect for beach lovers and water sports enthusiasts, with vibrant coastal towns and a lively atmosphere.

Considerations: Popular tourist season, so book accommodations well in advance.

Autumn (September to November):

Weather: Autumn offers pleasant temperatures, with cooler evenings and stunning fall foliage.

Advantages: Ideal for exploring cities, historical sites, and hiking trails without the summer heat.

Considerations: Crowds begin to thin out, but it's still advisable to book accommodations ahead.

Winter (December to February):

Weather: Winter can be chilly, especially in the mountainous regions, with occasional snowfall.

Advantages: Ideal for travelers seeking a peaceful, off-season experience and lower accommodation rates.

Considerations: Some attractions and services may have reduced hours or closures.

Your choice of season should align with your interests and activities. If you're a beach lover, summer might be the perfect time, while history enthusiasts may prefer the milder temperatures of spring or autumn.

Duration of Your Trip

Determining the length of your stay in Albania is the next crucial step in planning your trip. The duration can vary widely depending on your interests and the depth of exploration you desire. See some considerations:

Short Getaway (3-5 Days):

- A short trip is perfect for exploring a specific city or a couple of regions.

- Ideal for a quick escape to relax on the beach, explore historical towns, or enjoy a city break in Tirana.

Week-Long Adventure (7-10 Days):

- Allows you to delve deeper into the culture, history, and natural beauty of Albania.

- Suitable for a mix of coastal and inland exploration, including cities, beaches, and national parks.

Extended Exploration (2+ Weeks):

- Provides ample time to cover the entire country, including remote regions and off-the-beaten-path destinations.

- Ideal for travelers seeking a comprehensive experience and in-depth immersion in Albanian culture.

The duration of your trip should align with your travel style and interests. Keep in mind that Albania has a lot to offer, so the longer you can stay, the more you can uncover its hidden treasures.

Budgeting and Costs

Establishing a budget for your trip to Albania is essential for financial planning. Albania is known for offering great value for travelers, but it's still important to set clear financial boundaries. Some breakdown of typical expenses:

Accommodation:

- Budget travelers can find hostels and guesthouses for as low as $10-20 per night.

- Mid-range hotels and apartments typically cost between $40-100 per night.

- Luxury accommodations range from $100 and upwards.

Food:

- Dining at local restaurants and cafes is affordable, with meals averaging $5-15.

- Fine dining and upscale restaurants may cost $20-40 per person.

Transportation:

- Public transportation is budget-friendly, with bus and train fares generally ranging from $2-15 for longer journeys.

- Renting a car can cost anywhere from $30-100 per day, depending on the vehicle type.

Activities and Attractions:

- Entrance fees to museums and historical sites vary but are generally affordable, often less than $10.

- Activities such as hiking, water sports, and guided tours may have additional costs.

Miscellaneous:

- Allow for extra expenses such as souvenirs, travel insurance, and unexpected costs in your budget.

It's advisable to set a daily allowance based on your planned activities and preferences. Having a clear budget in mind will help you make informed decisions throughout your trip and ensure you stay within your financial comfort zone.

Travel Documentation and Visa Requirements

Before booking your trip, make sure you have all the necessary travel documents in order. These what you need to know:

Passport:

- Ensure your passport is valid for at least six months beyond your planned departure date from Albania.

Visa Requirements:

- Albania is part of the visa-free regime for many countries, including the United States, Canada, and most European countries. However, it's essential to check Albania's visa policy for your specific nationality before traveling.

Entry Requirements:

- Upon arrival in Albania, you may be required to provide proof of accommodation and sufficient funds for your stay.

Travel Insurance:

- Think about getting travel insurance that covers medical emergencies, vacation cancellations, and travel delays.

COVID-19 Considerations:

- Be aware of any COVID-19-related travel restrictions, including testing and quarantine requirements, which may change periodically.

Always verify visa and entry requirements with the Albanian embassy or consulate in your home country well in advance of your trip.

Choosing Your Mode of Transportation

Albania offers various transportation options for travelers, and your choice will depend on your itinerary and preferences:

Air Travel:

- Tirana International Airport (TIA) is the primary international gateway to Albania, with flights from major European cities.

- Other airports, such as Vlora International Airport, offer limited international flights.

- From Tirana, you can easily access other regions of the country by bus, train, or car.

Public Transportation:

- Buses and minibusses are the primary mode of long-distance public transportation, connecting major cities and towns.

- Trains are also available but may have limited routes.

- Public transportation is affordable and a popular choice among budget travelers.

Renting a Car:

- Renting a car allows for more flexibility and accessibility, especially if you plan to explore remote areas.

- Major rental car companies operate in Albania, and driving is on the right side of the road.

Taxis and Ride-Sharing:

- Taxis are readily available in cities and can be flagged down on the street or booked through ride-sharing apps like Uber and Bolt.

- Negotiate fares before starting your journey, as taxis may not always use meters.

Ferries:

- If you plan to explore Albania's coastal islands, consider taking ferries, which operate seasonally and connect the mainland to islands like Ksamil and Saranda.

Domestic Flights:

- For those with limited time, domestic flights within Albania are available, allowing for quick travel between major cities.

Cycling and Walking:

- Some areas, particularly in cities and along the coast, are suitable for cycling and walking. Tourist destinations provide bike rentals.

Your choice of transportation should align with your travel style, itinerary, and the regions you plan to explore. Albania's road network has improved in recent years, making it easier to travel by road, but be prepared for winding mountain roads in some areas.

Accommodation Options

Albania offers a range of accommodation options to suit every traveler's needs and budget:

Hotels:

- Hotels in Albania range from budget-friendly options to luxurious resorts.

- You'll find a variety of international hotel chains as well as charming boutique hotels in cities and tourist areas.

Hostels and Guesthouses:

- Budget-conscious travelers can choose from a selection of hostels and guesthouses, particularly in popular tourist destinations.

- Hostels often offer dormitory-style rooms, while guesthouses provide a more intimate experience.

Apartments and Vacation Rentals:

- Airbnb and other vacation rental platforms offer apartments and villas, ideal for families or travelers seeking more space and privacy.

Camping:

- Albania offers numerous camping sites, both along the coast and in national parks, for outdoor enthusiasts.

- Be sure to check the availability of amenities and facilities when planning a camping trip.

Historic Accommodations:

- Some historical towns, such as Gjirokastër and Berat, offer the unique opportunity to stay in renovated Ottoman-era houses, known as "kullë" or "konaks."

Beach Resorts:

- Along the Albanian Riviera, you'll find a selection of beachfront resorts, perfect for a relaxing coastal getaway.

Eco-Friendly Accommodations:

- Albania boasts eco-friendly and sustainable accommodations for travelers who prioritize environmental responsibility.

When choosing accommodations, consider factors such as location, amenities, and proximity to your planned activities. It's advisable to book accommodations well in advance, especially during the peak summer season, to secure the best options.

Creating Your Itinerary

Your itinerary is the roadmap to your Albanian adventure, and crafting a well-balanced plan ensures you make the most of your trip. This is how to create a memorable itinerary:

Research and Prioritize Destinations:

- Begin by researching Albania's top attractions and regions, such as Tirana, Berat, Gjirokastër, the Albanian Riviera, and national parks.

- Prioritize the destinations that align with your interests and activities.

Allocate Time:

- Determine the number of days you'll spend in each destination. For example, Tirana may require 2-3 days, while exploring the Albanian Riviera might take 4-5 days.

Consider Travel Time:

- Account for travel time between destinations, especially if you're relying on public transportation.

Balance Activities:

- Ensure a mix of cultural experiences, historical exploration, outdoor adventures, and relaxation.

Flexibility:

- Be sure to leave room in your schedule for last-minute additions and unplanned adventures.

Local Events and Festivals:

- Check if there are any local events or festivals during your visit, as these can provide unique cultural insights.

Day-to-Day Plans:

- Create a day-to-day breakdown of activities, accommodations, and meals.

- Be sure to include downtime for relaxation and exploration at your own pace.

Travel Resources:

- Utilize travel guides, blogs, and maps to gather information about each destination and its attractions.

Check Opening Hours:

- Verify the opening hours of museums, historical sites, and restaurants, as these may vary.

Local Cuisine:

- Plan to sample local Albanian cuisine at restaurants and markets, experiencing the flavors of the region.

Language and Communication

While English is commonly understood in urban areas and tourist destinations, learning a few basic phrases in Albanian can enhance your experience and interactions with locals. Some essential Albanian phrases include:

- *Hello: Tungjatjeta (Toon-gya-tye-ta)*

- *Goodbye: Mirupafshim (Meer-oo-pahf-shim)*

- *Please: Ju lutem (Yoo loo-tem)*

- *Thank you: Faleminderit (Fah-leh-min-deh-reet)*

- *Yes: Po (Poh)*

- *No: Jo (Yoh)*

- *Excuse me: Më falni (Muh fahl-nee)*

- *How much is this?: Sa kushton kjo? (Sah koo-shton kyo?)*

- *Where is...?: Ku është...? (Koo ush-tuh...?)*

- *I need help: Më duhet ndihmë (Muh doo-et ndeeh-muh)*

- *Water: Ujë (Ooy)*

- *Food: Ushqim (Oosh-qeem)*

- *Beer: Birrë (Beer-uh)*

- *Wine: Verë (Veh-ruh)*

- *Cheers!: Gëzuar! (Ge-zwahr!)*

Learning a few basic phrases not only makes your journey more enjoyable but also demonstrates respect for the local culture.

Health and Safety Preparations

The health and safety of travelers are paramount, and preparation is key to ensuring a worry-free trip. Here are some essential considerations:

Travel Insurance:

- Purchase comprehensive travel insurance that covers medical emergencies, trip cancellations, and travel disruptions.

Vaccinations:

- Consult your healthcare provider or travel clinic for up-to-date information on recommended vaccinations and health precautions for Albania.

Prescription Medications:

- If you take prescription medications, ensure you have an adequate supply for the duration of your trip and carry the necessary documentation.

Emergency Contacts:

- Carry a list of emergency contacts, including local authorities, your embassy or consulate, and contact information for your travel insurance provider.

Travel Health Kit:

- Pack a travel health kit with essentials such as first-aid supplies, over-the-counter medications, and personal hygiene items.

COVID-19 Considerations:

- Stay informed about any COVID-19-related requirements and restrictions that may apply during your trip.

Local Health Services:

- Familiarize yourself with the location of local hospitals, clinics, and pharmacies at your destinations.

Safety Precautions:

- Exercise standard safety precautions, such as safeguarding your belongings, avoiding poorly lit areas at night, and staying vigilant in crowded spaces.

Emergency Funds:

- Carry some emergency funds in a secure location, such as a money belt or hidden pouch, for unexpected expenses.

By taking these health and safety precautions, you can minimize risks and ensure a safer and more enjoyable trip to Albania.

Cultural Awareness and Etiquette

Albania has a rich cultural heritage, and being respectful of local customs and etiquette is essential. Some cultural tips include:

- **Dress Modestly**: When visiting religious sites, dress modestly by covering your shoulders and knees

- **Greetings**: Albanians typically greet with a kiss on both cheeks among friends and family. A handshake is common in formal settings.

- **Shoes Off**: When entering someone's home, it's traditional to take your shoes off.

- **Respect for Elders:** Show respect to older individuals in Albanian culture. Address them with "zoti" (Mr.) or "zonja" (Mrs.) followed by their last name.

- **Tipping:** Tipping is valued however not anticipated all the time. In restaurants, rounding up the bill is common.

- **Photography:** Consistently request consent prior to taking photographs of people, particularly in provincial regions.

- **Albanian Hospitality:** The warm hospitality of Albanians is well-known. Don't be surprised if you're invited to join locals for coffee or a meal.

- ***Religious Respect:*** When visiting churches or mosques, behave respectfully, and follow any posted rules.

Respecting local customs and being culturally aware will enhance your interactions with Albanians and leave a positive impression.

"Albania Travel Guide 2024" is an exhilarating undertaking, offering the chance to investigate a country with a rich social legacy, dazzling scenes, and warm cordiality. By carefully considering factors such as timing, budget, transportation, accommodation, and cultural awareness, you can ensure that your journey is filled with unforgettable experiences and cherished memories.

Remember that Albania is a country that rewards curiosity and adventurous spirits. Embrace the diversity of its regions, savor its cuisine, and immerse yourself in its history and traditions. With thoughtful planning and a spirit of exploration, your trip to Albania will undoubtedly be a remarkable and transformative adventure. So, prepare your bags and embark on a journey to discover the hidden treasures of Albania in 2024, a destination waiting to captivate your heart and soul.

Local Currency and Banking

Understanding the local currency and banking system is vital for a smooth trip. In Albania, the official currency is the Albanian Lek (ALL). Some tips for handling money include:

- ***Currency Exchange***: Exchange your currency to Albanian Lek at banks or exchange offices for better rates than at the airport. Major credit and debit cards are widely accepted in urban areas, but it's wise to carry some cash for smaller establishments and rural regions.

- ***ATMs:*** ATM machines are available in cities and larger towns. Visa and MasterCard are commonly accepted for withdrawals. Educate your bank regarding your itinerary items to keep away from card issues abroad.

- ***Currency Notes***: Familiarize yourself with Albanian currency notes to avoid confusion. The Lek comes in various denominations, including 200, 500, 1000, 2000, and 5000 Lekë.

- ***Tipping:*** Tipping is appreciated but not obligatory. In restaurants, consider rounding up the bill or leaving a small tip for good service.

- ***Safety Precautions:*** Keep your money and cards secure in a money belt, neck pouch, or RFID-blocking wallet to prevent theft or fraud.

Local Transportation and Getting Around

Navigating Albania's transportation system efficiently is essential to make the most of your trip. What you need to know are:

- ***Public Transportation***: Albania offers an extensive network of buses and minibusses that connect cities and towns. In Tirana, there's a trolleybus system, and taxis are readily available in urban areas. Familiarize yourself with local schedules and routes, which may vary by region.

- ***Renting a Car***: If you plan to explore beyond major cities, consider renting a car. Major car rental companies operate in Albania, but be prepared for mountainous terrain and winding roads, especially in rural areas.

- *Domestic Flights*: While Albania has a limited domestic flight network, it's an option for covering longer distances quickly. Some regional airports serve cities like Vlora and Saranda.

- *Ferries*: If you're interested in visiting Albania's islands, such as Ksamil and Saranda, look into ferry services. They operate seasonally and can be a unique travel experience.

- *Cycling*: Albania offers opportunities for cycling enthusiasts. Some cities have bike-sharing programs, and you can rent bicycles for exploring both urban and rural areas.

- *Walking*: Albanian cities, particularly historical districts, are pedestrian-friendly. Walking allows you to explore at a leisurely pace, discover hidden gems, and interact with locals.

Unique Albanian Experiences

In addition to well-known tourist attractions, consider adding unique experiences to your itinerary:

- ***Bunkers and Cold War History***: Explore the history of Albania's communist era by visiting the unique bunker sites and museums that tell the story of Enver Hoxha's regime.

- ***Traditional Albanian Music and Dance***: Attend a local music performance or a traditional Albanian dance show to immerse yourself in the country's rich cultural heritage.

- ***Raki Tasting***: Sample raki, Albania's traditional fruit brandy, at local distilleries or taverns, and learn about the cultural significance of this beverage.

- ***Hiking Adventures:*** Albania offers a wealth of hiking opportunities, from the Theth-Valbona trail to the Peaks of the Balkans trek. Consider incorporating a hiking adventure into your trip for stunning views and outdoor exploration.

- ***Homestays:*** Experience Albanian hospitality by staying in a local guesthouse or participating in homestays. This immersive experience allows you to connect with Albanian families and learn about their way of life.

- ***Wild Camping***: If you're an experienced camper, explore the option of wild camping in Albania's national parks for a unique adventure surrounded by nature.

- ***Local Markets***: Visit bustling local markets to experience the vibrant atmosphere, shop for unique souvenirs, and sample local street food.

Packing Essentials

Packing smartly ensures you're well-prepared for your trip. Here are some essentials to consider:

- ***Clothing***: Pack clothing suitable for the season and activities. Layers are helpful, as weather can vary. Don't forget swimwear for coastal regions.

- ***Footwear***: Comfortable walking shoes or hiking boots are essential, especially if you plan to explore national parks or trekking trails.

- ***Travel Adapters:*** Albania uses European-style Type C and Type F power outlets. Bring the appropriate travel adapter for your electronic devices.

- ***Reusable Water Bottle:*** Remain hydrated and decrease plastic waste by bringing a reusable *water bottle.* Tap water is generally safe in Tirana and larger cities, but consider using a filter or purchasing bottled water in rural areas.

- *Sun Protection:* Albania enjoys a Mediterranean climate, so pack sunscreen, sunglasses, and a wide-brimmed hat to protect yourself from the sun.

- *First-Aid Kit:* Include basic first-aid supplies like bandages, pain relievers, and any personal medications.

- *Language Guide:* Bring a pocket-sized Albanian phrasebook or language guide to help with communication.

- *Travel Locks:* Secure your luggage and valuables with travel locks to enhance security.

Environmental Considerations

Responsible travel is essential for preserving Albania's natural beauty and cultural heritage. Some eco-friendly travel tips include:

- *Reduce Plastic Waste:* Minimize your plastic usage by carrying a reusable shopping bag and using a reusable water bottle and utensils.

- *Respect Nature:* When hiking or exploring national parks, stick to marked trails to avoid damaging fragile ecosystems. Utilize the Leave No Trace principles.

- *Support Local Communities:* Buy locally made souvenirs and products to support the local economy. Visit neighborhood markets and eat at family-run eateries.

- *Dispose of Waste Properly:* Avoid littering and dispose of trash in designated bins.

- *Responsible Wildlife Viewing:* If you encounter wildlife, maintain a respectful distance and do not feed or disturb animals.

- *Conserve Water:* Be mindful of water usage, especially in regions where water may be scarce.

By practicing responsible and sustainable tourism, you can contribute to the preservation of Albania's natural and cultural heritage.

Staying Informed and Adaptability

Stay informed about current events, local regulations, and any travel advisories for Albania. Keep an eye on news and government websites for updates related to your trip. Flexibility is key, as unexpected situations can arise. Having a backup plan and being adaptable can help you navigate any challenges that may occur during your journey.

"Albania Travel Guide 2024" unveils exciting endeavor, offering a blend of natural beauty, cultural richness, and warm hospitality. By considering local currency, transportation options, unique experiences, packing essentials, environmental responsibility, and staying informed, you can ensure a memorable and fulfilling journey. Albania beckons with its hidden treasures and unique charm, ready to captivate the adventurous traveler's heart and soul.

CHAPTER THREE

Seven (7) Days Itinerary Plan

Planning a 7-day plan for your vacation to Albania in 2024 is an intriguing concept. "Albania Travel Guide 2024" will help you make the most of your week-long vacation by showcasing the country's numerous attractions, natural beauty, historical places, and cultural experiences.

The Best of Albania in 2024

A week in Albania is an excellent opportunity to discover this Balkan gem's breathtaking scenery, rich history, and kind friendliness. This 7-day itinerary has been carefully crafted to provide a well-rounded experience, taking you on a journey through Albania's diverse regions, from the bustling capital city of Tirana to the pristine beaches of the Albanian Riviera, and from the ancient cities of Berat and Gjirokastr to the serene beauty of the country's national parks.

Day 1: Arrival in Tirana

- ***Morning***: Arrive at Tirana International Airport (TIA), Albania's principal gateway. After passing through immigration and customs, proceed to your chosen hotel in Tirana, Albania's dynamic capital city.

- ***Afternoon***: Begin your journey of Tirana with a visit to Skanderbeg Square, the city's major square named for Gjergj Kastrioti Skanderbeg, the national hero. Admire Skanderbeg's horse monument and the beautiful structures that surround the area.

- ***Evening***: Take a stroll through the vibrant Blloku area, which was originally reserved for Communist Party elites. It is now the city's most stylish district, featuring trendy clubs, restaurants, and shops. At a local eatery, try your first taste of Albanian food.

Day 2: Tirana's Cultural and Historical Sights

- ***Morning:*** Dive into Tirana's rich history by visiting the National Historical Museum, which displays a massive collection spanning Albania's history from ancient times to the present. Don't overlook the amazing mosaic on the facade.

- *Afternoon*: Visit the Bunk'Art 2 museum, an underground bunker turned modern art space. This one-of-a-kind museum offers insights about Albania's Communist period and its influence on the country.

- *Evening*: Take in the bustling atmosphere of Tirana's Pyramid, a contentious landmark that has become a favorite hangout for residents. Climb to the peak for a 360-degree view of the city. In the evening, dine at a local restaurant on a traditional Albanian dinner.

Day 3: Berat, The City with a Thousand Windows.

- *Morning*: Depart for Berat, a lovely town renowned as the "City of a Thousand Windows" because to its well-preserved Ottoman-era architecture. Explore Mangalem's historic area, a UNESCO World Heritage Site, with its characteristic white buildings.

- *Afternoon*: Visit Berat Castle, a historic stronghold built on a hill above the town. Explore the Onufri Museum inside the castle, which displays a remarkable collection of religious art, including works by the great iconographer Onufri.

- *Evening*: Enjoy a typical Albanian supper at a local restaurant within the castle walls, with spectacular views of Berat and the surrounding countryside.

Day 4: Gjirokastr - The Stone City

- *Morning*: Depart for Gjirokastr, another UNESCO World Heritage Site called as "The Stone City." Explore the well-preserved medieval town, which is distinguished by stone homes with characteristic slate roofs.

- *Afternoon*: Visit Gjirokastr Castle, a huge stronghold that houses the Gjirokastr Ethnographic Museum. This museum gives insights into the region's history, culture, and traditional way of life.

- *Evening*: Enjoy a traditional Albanian supper at a local restaurant in Gjirokastr, where you can sample local delicacies like qofte (meatballs) and byrek (savory pastry).

Day 5: The Albanian Riviera - Dhërmi and Jale Beaches

- *Morning*: Depart for the magnificent Albanian Riviera, known for its pristine beaches and crystal-clear seas. Your first destination is Dhrmi Beach, a charming coastal community famed for its magnificent beaches and rugged cliffs.

- *Afternoon*: Continue to Jale Beach, where you may relax on the sandy sands or swim in the blue seas. The Albanian Riviera is a great area for beachgoers to relax and enjoy the Mediterranean sun.

- *Evening*: Spend the night in one of the gorgeous beachfront lodgings in Dhrmi or Jale and dine at a seaside restaurant, tasting fresh seafood dishes while listening to the relaxing sound of the waves.

Day 6: Llogara Pass and Himara

- *Morning*: Drive via the magnificent Llogara Pass, a hilly stretch of road with panoramic views of the Ionian Sea and the coastal cliffs below. Take in the breathtaking scenery and snap some great shots.

- *Afternoon*: Arrive at Himara, a seaside town noted for its magnificent beaches and ancient buildings. Explore Himara Castle, set on a hill above the town, and the neighboring Old Village, with its small cobblestone lanes.

- *Evening*: Dine at a Himara seaside restaurant, where you may savor fresh seafood and authentic Albanian cuisine while watching the sunset over the sea.

Day 7: Apollonia Archaeological Park and Return to Tirana

- *Morning*: Depart Himara for Apollonia Archaeological Park, an ancient city built in the sixth century BC. Explore the well-preserved ruins, which include the Temple of Artemis and the Odeon.

- *Afternoon:* After your excursion to Apollonia, return to Tirana and do some last-minute gift shopping or relax in a local park.

- *Evening*: Finish your adventure with a goodbye supper in Tirana, reflecting about your fantastic week in Albania and relishing the tastes of Albanian cuisine.

Additional Tips and Considerations

- *Travel Time*: While this route gives a comprehensive picture of Albania, consider extending your trip to include other locations such as the northern highlands, Prespa National Park, or the historic city of Butrint in the south.

- *Local Cuisine*: Along the shore, try traditional Albanian cuisine like tave kosi (baked lamb with yogurt), frges (pepper and tomato stew), and fresh fish.

- *Local Festivals*: Check to see if any local festivals or events are taking place during your stay, since they can give unique cultural experiences as well as opportunity to engage with locals.

- *Language*: While English is widely spoken in cities and tourist regions, learning a few basic Albanian words will improve your experience and interactions with locals.

- *Safety*: Albania is usually regarded as safe for visitors, although basic measures, such as keeping your possessions secure and avoiding poorly lit places at night, should be taken.

- *Photography*: Ask for permission before photographing persons, especially in rural regions, and respect residents' privacy.

This 7-day tour provides a look into Albania's unique tapestry of history, culture, and natural beauty. It's intended to deliver a well-rounded experience, but you may customize it to your specific interests and tastes. Albania in 2024 is a place ready to thrill and inspire, providing a week of unforgettable activities and discoveries.

CHAPTER FOUR

Top Attractions To Visit In Albania

Albania is noted for its mountainous coastline along the Ionian and Adriatic Seas, as well as old archaeological sites and bustling towns. Albania entices visitors in 2024 with its beauty and distinct combination of Mediterranean and Balkan cultures. Let's go on an excursion to explore the top attractions that make Albania such an intriguing location for your next vacation.

Tirana, Albania's Capital

Tirana, Albania's lively capital, is your entry to the country's rich history and modern culture. Begin your trip in Skanderbeg Square, named for Gjergj Kastrioti Skanderbeg, a national hero. The area is embellished with a large statue of Skanderbeg on horseback.

The *Et'hem Bey Mosque*, a masterpiece of Albanian architecture, is one of Tirana's most outstanding structures. Its elaborate paintings and exquisite interiors stand in stark contrast to the busy metropolis beyond.

Visit *Tirana's New Bazaar, Pazari i Ri,* where residents congregate to buy fresh vegetables, Albanian specialties, and one-of-a-kind handicrafts. Try traditional Albanian coffee and street cuisine like "qebapa" (grilled pork).

The *National Historical Museum* provides an insight into Albania's past. It has a large collection spanning the country's history, from ancient Illyria to the current period.

Bunk'Art 2 is a one-of-a-kind subterranean museum built in a decommissioned nuclear bunker. Through art and antiques, learn about Albania's turbulent past throughout the Communist era.

Don't pass up the chance to climb the Pyramid of Tirana, a renowned but contentious Communist-era landmark. It offers sweeping views of the city.

Tirana: Albania Capital City

Berat - "City of a Thousand Windows"

Berat, also known as the "City of a Thousand Windows," is a UNESCO World Heritage Site. Its distinctive Ottoman architecture and well-preserved historic area, *Mangalem*, bear witness to its illustrious history.

The *Berat Castle*, positioned on a hill, provides stunning views of the town below. Explore the grounds of the castle and pay a visit to the Onufri Museum, which features religious icons and artworks by the famed Albanian iconographer Onufri.

Gjirokastr - The "Stone City"

Gjirokastr, another UNESCO World Heritage Site, is also known as the "Stone City." Its well-preserved Ottoman-era architecture, with characteristic slate roofs, makes it a living museum.

The *Gjirokastr Castle*, a large fortification, contains the *Gjirokastr Ethnographic Museum*, which provides insights into the region's history and traditional way of life.

The stone city

The Albanian Riviera - Seaside Paradise

The *Albanian Riviera*, along the Ionian Ocean, offers immaculate sea shores, completely clear waters, and a casual environment. *Dhërmi*, with its wonderful sea shores and rough precipices, is a must-visit. Proceed to Jale Beach, an unexpected, yet invaluable treasure, for a calmer seaside experience.

Remember to investigate the *Llogara Pass*, a grand mountain street that offers all-encompassing perspectives on the ocean and the seaside precipices beneath.

Seaside Paradise

Llogara Pass - A Precipitous Wonderland

The **Llogara Pass** isn't simply a street; it's an excursion through a portion of Albania's most stunning scenes. This bumpy stretch offers all-encompassing perspectives on the Ionian Ocean and the Albanian Riviera beneath.

Stop at one of the perspectives along the pass to take in the staggering vistas, catch vital photographs, and partake in a cookout in the midst of the normal magnificence.

Apollonia Archaeological Park - Ancient Splendor

Apollonia, established in the sixth century BC, is an old city with a rich history. Investigate its archeological park, which incorporates the vestiges of the *Temple of Artemis* and the *Odeon*, a Roman-time theater.

Krujë - The Brave City

Krujë, known as the "Brave City," is renowned for its job in Albania's obstruction against the Ottoman Domain. Visit the Krujë Castle, which offers all encompassing perspectives on the town and houses the **Skanderbeg Museum**, devoted to the public legend.

Shkodër - Social Center in the North

Shkodër, situated in the north, is a social center point with a rich history. Investigate the Rozafa Castle, which offers all-encompassing perspectives on Lake Shkodër and the encompassing scenes.

The palace has its own legend, including a heartbreaking story of penance and treachery.

The Marubi Public Gallery of Photography is an extraordinary fascination in Shkodër, exhibiting a tremendous assortment of verifiable photos that give a visual excursion through Albania's past.

Valbona Valley - Elevated Serenity

Valbona Valley is a perfect normal marvel concealed in the Albanian Alps. It's an open air devotee's heaven, offering climbing trails through thick timberlands, past knolls, and to shocking perspectives.

Theth - A Far off Mountain Village

For a valid mountain experience, dare to Theth, a far off town settled in the Albanian Alps. Investigate the Lock-in Tower, an image of the district, and witness the conventional "blood fight" compromise process.

Butrint - Antiquated Archeological Site

Butrint, an UNESCO World Legacy Site, is an old city with a set of experiences going back more than 2,500 years. Investigate its archeological site, which incorporates a very much saved Roman theater, old sanctuaries, and a Byzantine baptistery.

Ksamil - A Cut of Paradise

Ksamil, situated in the south, is a waterfront jewel with unblemished sea shores and completely clear waters. Its nearness to the Butrint Public Park makes it an ideal objective for ocean side darlings and nature fans the same.

Shëngjin - Coastline Escape

Shëngjin, a waterfront town along the Adriatic Ocean, offers delightful sea shores and a casual environment. It's a fantastic spot to loosen up and partake in the Mediterranean sun.

Prespa Public Park - A Characteristic Oasis

Prespa Public Park, arranged in the southeast, is a sanctuary for birdwatchers and nature sweethearts.

Investigate Lake Prespa and its assorted environments, including wetlands and timberlands.

Dajti Mountain Public Park - A Characteristic Retreat

Dajti Mountain Public Park, simply a short drive from Tirana, offers a characteristic retreat with climbing trails, rich woods, and all-encompassing perspectives on the capital and the encompassing scenes.

Vlora - Verifiable Seaport

Vlora, a verifiable seaport on the Adriatic Ocean, is known for its wonderful sea shores and its part in Albania's battle for freedom. Visit the Independence Monument and partake in the seafront promenade.

Shala Waterway - A Secret Gem

The Shala River, in the northern Albanian Alps, is an unlikely treasure known for its emerald-hued waters and sensational gullies. Go on a boat outing on the stream and investigate the caverns and cascades en route.

Qeparo - A Waterfront Gem

Qeparo, a seaside town in the Albanian Riviera, flaunts staggering sea shores and enchanting stone houses.

Investigate the town's noteworthy engineering and loosen up on the quiet shores.

Koman Lake - A Peaceful Escape

Koman Lake, encompassed by rough mountains, is an unspoiled objective for a boat trip. Voyage through the tight fjords and take in the unblemished magnificence of the Albanian wild.

Berat Palace - A Verifiable Gem

The Berat Castle, an UNESCO World Legacy Site, is an old fortification that disregards the town of Berat. Investigate its very much safeguarded engineering and take in all encompassing perspectives on the town and the Osum Waterway.

The Blue Eye - A Characteristic Wonder

The Blue Eye is a characteristic spring with perfectly clear blue waters that appear to come from the profundities of the earth. It's a dreamlike and hypnotizing sight for nature lovers.

Gjipe Ocean side - A Secret Paradise

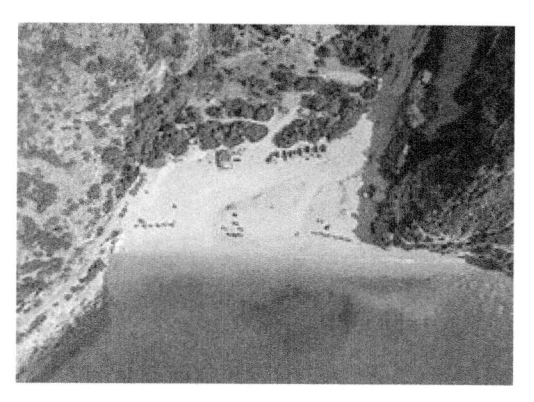

Gjipe Beach, open by climbing or boat, is a confined heaven with a flawless ocean side and sensational precipices. It's an optimal spot for those looking for serenity and experience.

Lëkurësi Palace - Sitting above Saranda

Lëkurësi Castle in Saranda offers all-encompassing perspectives on the town, the Ionian Ocean, and the close by Greek island of Corfu.

It's an extraordinary spot to watch the dusk over the ocean.

Lekuresi Cloister - A Profound Retreat

The Lekuresi Monastery, situated close to Saranda, is a quiet and verifiable site. Investigate the cloister's engineering, partake in the serene environmental elements, and take in perspectives on Saranda Narrows.

Korçë - The City of Serenades

Korçë, frequently alluded to as the "City of Songs," is known for its rich social legacy and customs. Visit the National Gallery of Archaic Art and investigate the town's energetic climate.

Koman Hydroelectric Power Plant - Designing Marvel

The Koman Hydroelectric Power Plant isn't simply a designing wonder yet additionally offers a shocking excursion through the Albanian Alps. Take a ship ride on Koman Lake to see the value in its emotional fjords and rough scenes.

Divjaka-Karavasta Public Park - Wetland Wonderland

Divjaka-Karavasta Public Park is a wetland heaven along the Adriatic Ocean. Investigate the unblemished sea shores, tidal ponds, and various bird species that call this park home.

Kukës - History and Nature

Kukës, in the upper east, is a town with a rich history and admittance to regular miracles.

Visit the Museum of Paganism and close by attractions like the Drini River.

Pogradec - Serene Lakeside

Pogradec, arranged on the shores of Lake Ohrid, is known for its tranquil vibe and dazzling lake sees. Investigate the town's promenade and loosen up by the lake.

Bënja Warm Pools - Unwinding Oasis

THERMAL POOLS

The Bënja Warm Pools offer a characteristic spa experience in the southern city of Përmet. Absorb the warm, mineral-rich waters and partake in the picturesque environmental elements.

With its various attractions, Albania in 2024 responsibilities explorers a trip stacked up with social exposures, outdoors encounters, and depictions of tranquility by the sea or in the mountains. Whether you're researching old metropolitan regions, relaxing on wonderful beaches, or plunging into Albania's rich history, this enchanting country offers something that would be useful for each kind of explorer. Get ready to set out on an unprecedented encounter through the top attractions of Albania, where each area relates a record of inheritance and greatness.

CHAPTER FIVE
Beaches In Albania

Investigating the Perfect Sea shores of Albania in 2024

Envision a shoreline where the perfectly clear waters of the Ionian and Adriatic Oceans touch brilliant sands, and tough precipices outline beautiful bayous.

This is the Albanian Riviera, a stretch of shoreline that stays quite possibly of Europe's trick of the trade. In 2024, Albania's sea shores are ready to offer explorers an untainted heaven, with a scope of encounters from unwinding to experience.

Dhërmi Beach - The Jewel of the Riviera

Dhërmi Beach, frequently hailed as the "Pearl of the Albanian Riviera," is a stunning seaside diamond. Its immaculate waters and rough bluffs make a sensational differentiation against the brilliant sands. Dhërmi offers a blend of laid-back ocean front bars and extravagance resorts.

-*What to Do*: Loosen up around the ocean, swim in the purplish blue waters, and investigate close by caves and secret bays. Dhërmi is likewise an extraordinary spot for swimming and jumping.

Jale Beach - Peaceful Escape

Jale Beach, found a short drive from Dhërmi, is a serene getaway portrayed by its untainted magnificence. It's a serene sanctuary for those looking for isolation in the midst of nature.

- *What to Do*: Partake in the harmony and calm, luxuriate in the sun, and go for relaxed strolls along the shore. Jale is likewise a famous spot for setting up camp and picnicking.

Ksamil - The Ionian Gem

Ksamil, on the southern Albanian Riviera, brags a few the most charming sea shores in Albania. With its reasonable blue waters and close by islands, it's frequently contrasted with tropical heavens.

- *What to Do*: Investigate the sea shores and islands of Ksamil, like Three Islands and Monastery Island. Swimming and boat trips are well known exercises here.

Gjipe Beach - A Secret Paradise

Gjipe Beach, open exclusively by boat or a difficult climb, is a secret heaven settled between transcending bluffs. Its separated area adds to its charm, making it a number one among experience searchers.

- **What to Do:** Climb to Gjipe Beach for dazzling perspectives or go on a boat outing from Dhërmi. You can likewise camp near the ocean and partake in the peaceful environmental elements.

Drymades Beach - The Surfer's Haven

Drymades Beach, close to Dhërmi, is known for its ideal circumstances for water sports, especially windsurfing and kitesurfing. The consistent breezes and wonderful landscape make it a #1 among surf lovers.

- *What to Do*: Have a go at windsurfing or kitesurfing with examples from nearby teachers. Loosen up on the sandy ocean side and partake in the ocean front bars.

Palasë Beach - Segregated Beauty

Palasë Beach, situated among Dhërmi and Vuno, is an unexpected, yet invaluable treasure that offers a more separated ocean side insight. The encompassing olive forests and lavish vegetation add to its appeal.

- *What to Do*: Investigate the serene environmental elements, go for long strolls along the ocean side, or partake in a peaceful outing. Palasë is ideally suited for a tranquil retreat.

Qeparo Beach - Waterfront Paradise

Qeparo Beach, with its perfectly clear waters and beautiful setting, is a waterfront heaven that offers both unwinding and regular magnificence. It's isolated into two sections: Lower Qeparo and Upper Qeparo.

- *What to Do*: Visit both Lower and Upper Qeparo to investigate the sea shores, olive forests, and enchanting towns. Take in all encompassing perspectives from Upper Qeparo.

Borsh Beach - Longest Ocean side in Albania

Borsh Beach, extending for north of seven kilometers, is the longest ocean side in Albania. It offers a blend of rocks and sand, making it an incredible objective for long strolls along the shore.

- ***What to Do***: Stroll along the broad ocean side, swim free waters, and appreciate neighborhood fish in ocean front eateries.

Livadhi Beach - Picturesque Beauty

Livadhi Beach, close to Himara, is known for its picturesque excellence and serene air. The background of pine-covered slopes and the turquoise ocean makes a staggering difference.

- *What to Do*: Loosen up on the ocean front, investigate the close by slopes, and appreciate new fish at nearby cafés.

10. Vuno Beach - Tranquil Hideaway

Vuno Beach, near Dhërmi, is a quiet hideout that offers harmony and serenity away from the groups. It's an ideal spot for those looking for isolation.

- *What to Do*: Partake in the calm ocean side, investigate the enchanting town of Vuno, and take in sees from the close by slopes.

Golem Beach - Family-Friendly

Golem Beach, close to Durrës, is known for its family-accommodating environment and various ocean front hotels. It's a well known objective for the two local people and travelers.

- **What to Do**: Loosen up on the ocean front, take part in water sports, and investigate close by attractions like the Durrës Amphitheater.

Karaburun Landmass - Immaculate Beauty

The Karaburun Peninsula, a safeguarded region, offers immaculate magnificence and tough shorelines. It's a sanctuary for nature darlings and those looking for remote sea shores.

- *What to Do*: Climb along the landmass' paths, investigate stowed away bays, and find the region's different widely varied vegetation.

Velipoja Beach - Northern Escape

Velipoja Beach, in the north, is a wide sandy ocean side known for its shallow waters and family-accommodating air. It's a famous objective for Northern Albanians.

- ***What to Do***: Partake in the shallow waters, go on a boat outing on the Buna Waterway, and investigate the close by tidal pond.

Shëngjin Ocean side - Adriatic Serenity

Shëngjin Beach, along the Adriatic Ocean, offers a casual climate and a long promenade fixed with bistros and eateries. It's an incredible spot to loosen up.

- *What to Do*: Walk around the promenade, swim in the quiet waters, and relish fish dishes in ocean front restaurants.

Dhërmi Secret Sea shores - Stowed away Charms

While Dhërmi's fundamental ocean side is notable, the region likewise brags a number secret bays and mystery sea shores. These concealed diamonds offer disconnection and regular excellence.

- **What to Do**: Investigate the mystery sea shores by going on short climbs or boat outings from Dhërmi.

Bunec Beach - Quiet Retreat

Bunec Beach, close to Jale, is a quiet retreat known for its quiet waters and lovely environmental factors. It's an optimal spot for a tranquil ocean side day.

- **What to Do**: Loosen up near the ocean, swim in the delicate waters, and partake in a tranquil day by the ocean.

Vuno-Mirror Beach - Confined Oasis

Vuno-Mirror Beach, settled among Jale and Dhermi, is a segregated desert garden with perfectly clear waters.

It's an ideal break from the groups.

- *What to Do*: Go through a loosening up day on the ocean front, swim free waters, and partake in the quiet climate.

Shën Jani Bay - Stowed away Treasure

Shën Jani Bay, close to Jale, is a secret fortune that offers a tranquil ocean side insight.

The inlet is encircled by rich vegetation and olive forests.

- *What to Do*: Loosen up around the ocean, take in the regular magnificence, and investigate the close by open country.

Spille Beach - Tranquil Getaway

Spille Beach, near Durrës, is a tranquil escape known for its quiet waters and family-accommodating environment.

It's an extraordinary spot for a roadtrip from the city.

- *What to Do*: Loosen up on the sandy ocean side, swim in the delicate waters, and appreciate nearby fish in ocean front cafés.

Porto Palermo - Notable Beach

Porto Palermo, close to Himara, consolidates regular excellence with authentic interest.

It includes an enchanting cove with perfectly clear waters and the interesting Porto Palermo Castle.

- *What to Do*: Investigate the palace, swim in the cove, and partake in a day of unwinding and investigation.

Zvërnec Island - Serene Retreat

Zvërnec Island, close to Vlora, is a serene retreat known for its sandy ocean side and the Zvërnec Monastery.

The island's tranquil climate is ideally suited for a quiet escape.

- *What to Do*: Visit the cloister, loosen up on the ocean front, and go for a relaxed walk around the island.

Gjiri I Grames - Quiet Bay

Gjiri I Grames, close to Karaburun Landmass, is a quiet cove with quiet waters and normal magnificence.

It's a secret spot for those hoping to get away from the groups.

- **What to Do**: Partake in the quietness, swim in the cove, and investigate the encompassing precipices and caverns.

Zvernec Beach - Quiet Escape

Zvernec Beach, close to Vlora, offers a quiet departure with its quiet waters and regular environmental elements. It's an extraordinary spot for a peaceful day by the ocean.

- **What to Do**: Loosen up on the ocean front, swim in the delicate waters, and investigate the close by Zvërnec Island.

Gjipe Secret Beach - Stowed away Gem

Gjipe Secret Beach, open exclusively by boat or a difficult climb, is an unlikely treasure settled between bluffs. Its separated area makes it a number one among courageous explorers.

- **What to Do**: Climb to the mystery ocean side for dazzling perspectives or go on a boat outing from Dhërmi. You can likewise camp on the ocean front and partake in the peaceful environmental elements.

Llamani Beach - Disconnected Beauty

Llamani Beach, close to Jale, is a disconnected marvel that offers a peaceful ocean side insight. Encircled by precipices and lavish vegetation, it's an ideal spot for unwinding.

- **What to Do:** Partake in the harmony and calm, swim free waters, and go for comfortable strolls along the shore.

These sea shores are only a brief look at Albania's beach front marvels. In 2024, Albania's perfect shores offer an opportunity to get away from the groups and find pristine magnificence. Whether you're looking for unwinding, water sports, or experience, Albania's sea shores bring something to the table for each explorer, promising an important ocean side excursion along the shores of the Ionian and Adriatic Oceans.

CHAPTER SIX
Albania Delicacy

Savoring the Flavors of Albania in 2024

Setting out on an excursion through Albania implies finding its shocking scenes as well as enjoying its one of a kind and delicious cooking. Albanian food is an impression of the country's different social legacy, mixing Mediterranean and Balkan impacts with a dash of the intriguing. In 2024, Albania's culinary scene offers an enticing exhibit of flavors and dishes that will leave each food fan hankering for more.

Tavë Kosi - The Public Dish

Tavë Kosi, a darling Albanian dish, is many times thought about the country's public food. It's an encouraging goulash produced using sheep or chicken, yogurt, and eggs, all prepared to velvety flawlessness. The blend of delicate meat and tart yogurt makes a rich and fulfilling flavor.

Byrek - Flavorful Baked good Delight

Byrek, an exquisite baked good, is a staple of Albanian cooking. Slight layers of mixture are loaded up with various fixings, like cheddar, spinach, or minced meat, making a flavorful tidbit or feast.

Byrek is frequently delighted in with yogurt or ayran, a yogurt-based drink.

Qofte - Delightful Meatballs

Qofte, or meatballs, are a famous road food and solace dish in Albania. Ground meat, normally a blend of hamburger and sheep, is prepared with spices and flavors, then, at that point, formed into patties and barbecued flawlessly.

Presented with new bread or in a pita, qofte is a tasty and filling choice.

Fërgesë - Peppers and Cheddar Delight

Fërgesë, a good dish, consolidates green and red peppers with tomatoes, onions, and nearby cheddar. It's frequently presented with hotdogs or meat and cooked gradually to foster rich flavors.

Fërgesë grandstands the utilization of privately created dairy items and new vegetables.

Tave Dheu - Mountain Delicacy

Tave Dheu, otherwise called "Mountain Dish," is a delightful mixture of sheep or goat meat slow-cooked with wild spices and flavors.

This provincial dish catches the substance of Albania's bumpy districts and is a genuine pleasure for meat sweethearts.

Baklava - Wonderful Sensation

Baklava, a sweet cake made of layers of filo batter loaded up with nuts and improved with syrup, is a cherished pastry in Albania. It's not unexpected served on unique events and festivities, displaying the country's sweet tooth.

Pite - Layered Pie Goodness

Pite, like byrek, is a layered pie with different fillings.

Whether it's loaded up with spinach, cheddar, or pumpkin, pite is a flexible dish that can be delighted in as a tidbit, starter, or principal course.

Japrak - Stuffed Plant Leaves

Japrak, or stuffed plant leaves, is a Mediterranean-propelled dish famous in Albania.

Grape leaves are loaded down with a combination of rice, ground meat, spices, and flavors, then cooked until delicate. Japrak is frequently presented with yogurt or a tomato-based sauce.

Kos - Reviving Yogurt Drink

Kos, a customary yogurt drink, is a reviving method for chilling off on a hot Albanian day.

It's like buttermilk and is much of the time appreciated close by exquisite dishes like byrek or tavë kosi.

Qumeshtor - Smooth Dessert

Qumeshtor, a smooth pastry produced using milk, sugar, and cornstarch, is a consoling treat cherished by Albanians, all things considered. It's frequently decorated with a sprinkle of cinnamon and served chilled.

Peqë - Fig Dessert

Peqë, a remarkable sweet, highlights dried figs loaded down with pecans and cloves, then, at that point, bubbled in a sugar syrup.

This sweet delicacy catches the substance of Albanian cordiality.

Raki - Customary Albanian Spirit

Raki, a solid grape liquor, is a conventional Albanian soul frequently presented as a token of neighborliness.

It's tasted previously or after a feast and is accepted to help processing.

Gliko - Saved Natural product Delight

Gliko, or saved natural product, is a sweet treat made by stewing natural products like cherries, figs, or quince in sugar syrup.

It's a famous custom made dessert frequently presented with some Turkish espresso.

Flija - Layered Flapjack Perfection

Flija, a remarkable flapjack like dish, is made by pouring slight layers of player over one another and cooking them on an open fire. It's frequently delighted in with honey, yogurt, or jam and is a unique treat at get-togethers.

Pasha Qofte - Easter Meatballs

Pasha Qofte, or Easter meatballs, are a conventional dish ready during Easter festivals.

They are produced using a combination of sheep, rice, and different flavors, representing the delight of Easter.

Tarator - Chilled Cucumber Soup

Tarator, a chilled cucumber and yogurt soup, is a reviving dish ideal for warm late spring days.

It's carefully prepared with garlic, dill, and pecans, making a magnificent equilibrium of flavors.

Suxhuk - Sweet Sausage

Suxhuk, a sweet hotdog produced using a combination of pecans, sugar, and flavors, is a well-known Albanian bite.

It's frequently delighted in with areas of strength for some or tea.

Tavë Elbasani - Elbasan Casserole

Tavë Elbasani, named after the city of Elbasan, is a generous dish made with sheep, yogurt, and eggs.

It's a tasty dish that grandstands the nation's adoration for sheep.

Trilece - Smooth Cake Delight

Trilece, a smooth treat cake, is a sweet guilty pleasure produced using three sorts of milk: dense, vanished, and normal milk.

A delicious treat softens in your mouth.

Petulla - Broiled Batter Delight

Petulla, rotisserie batter wastes, are a well-known Albanian tidbit frequently delighted in with powdered sugar or honey. They're fresh outwardly and delicate within, making them overpowering.

Pogaqe - Olive Oil Bread

Pogaqe, a sort of bread made with olive oil, is a staple in Albanian families.

It's frequently seasoned with spices and filled in as a backup to dinners.

Gjellë me Arra - Pecan Stew

Gjellë me Arra, or pecan stew, is a rich and generous dish made with meat and walnuts. It's a tasty creation that exhibits the utilization of nuts in Albanian food.

Kackavall - Nearby Cheese

Kackavall, a semi-hard sheep's milk cheddar, is a typical fixing in Albanian cooking. It's not unexpected barbecued and filled in as a side dish or utilized as a filling in dishes like byrek.

Përime - Salted Vegetables

Përime, or salted vegetables, are a famous backup to numerous Albanian dinners.

They add a tart and crunchy component to the eating experience.

Fërgesë e Tiranës - Tirana's Fërgesë

Fërgesë e Tiranës, or Tirana's Fërgesë, is a variety of the exemplary dish made with green and red peppers, tomatoes, onions, and nearby cheddar.

It's a delightful interpretation of a dearest Albanian dish.

Kanojët - Albanian Cannoli

Kanojët, Albanian cannoli, are a great treat produced using a seared baked good shell loaded up with sweet ricotta cheddar, sugar, and vanilla. They're a sweet closure of any Albanian feast.

Dashuria - Albanian Hospitality

In Albania, food isn't just about food; it's an image of neighborliness and kinship. Albanians invest wholeheartedly in imparting their culinary customs to visitors, and each dinner is a challenge to relish the glow and liberality of the way of life.

Where to Appreciate Albanian Cuisine

While visiting Albania in 2024, you'll track down various cafés, bistros, and neighborhood diners where you can appreciate these delightful dishes. The absolute best places to encounter Albanian cooking include:

- ***Conventional Kitchens***: Search out neighborhood, family-run cafés and customary kitchens for a bona fide taste of Albanian home cooking.

- ***Beach front Restaurants***: Along the dazzling shore, you'll find fish eateries serving newly got fish and other fish luxuries.

- ***Road Food Stalls***: Make sure to road food slows down for light meals of exquisite pies, meatballs, and sweet treats.

- ***Nearby Markets***: Investigate neighborhood markets and attempt new produce, cheeses, olives, from there, the sky is the limit. You could get a few fixings to reproduce Albanian dishes at home.

- ***Memorable Cities***: In urban communities like Tirana, Berat, and Gjirokastër, you'll find cafés offering a mix of customary Albanian and current Mediterranean food.

Dietary Considerations

Albanian cooking offers choices for different dietary inclinations and limitations. Veggie lover and vegetarian dishes are accessible, frequently including new vegetables, grains, and sans dairy choices. Numerous Albanian dishes can be custom fitted to oblige explicit dietary necessities, so make it a point to for changes while eating out.

Culinary Experiences

To completely submerge yourself in Albanian food, consider participating in cooking classes or culinary visits. These encounters offer an involved way to deal with finding out about nearby fixings and methods while partaking in the joy of getting ready and tasting legitimate dishes.

Espresso Culture

Albanians view their espresso in a serious way, and espresso culture assumes a huge part in day to day existence. Partake in areas of strength for some espresso, frequently presented with a glass of water, at a neighborhood bistro or as a component of a customary espresso service.

In ''Albania Travel Guide 2024'', the culinary scene vows to be a brilliant excursion of flavors, where customary recipes and imaginative turns meet up to make a lively and different feasting experience. As you investigate this wonderful nation, appreciating its heavenly food is a fundamental piece of figuring out its rich culture and friendliness. Whether you're enjoying the public dish, Tavë Kosi, tasting areas of strength for on, or examining sweet baklava, Albania's cooking will have an enduring impact on your taste buds and your heart.

CHAPTER SEVEN
Nightlife In Albania

Albania's nightlife scene has been developing quick recently, offering a variety of choices for evening people and party lovers. In this "Albania Travel Guide 2024", we will dive into the energetic nightlife of the country, from the clamoring city areas of interest to the seaside ocean side clubs, furnishing you with a thrilling look into the country's evening amusement.

Encountering the Nightlife of Albania

At the point when the sun sets over Albania, the nation wakes up with an energy and dynamic quality that is difficult to stand up to. Albanian nightlife has gone through a change lately, and today it offers a different scope of choices for those looking for energy in the evening. From the humming capital of Tirana to the vivacious beach front towns, Albania's nightlife scene guarantees paramount nights loaded up with music, moving, and a sprinkle of Mediterranean pizazz.

Tirana - The Nightlife Capital

Tirana, the capital city of Albania, is the focal point of the nation's nightlife. As of late, it has arisen as a dynamic and cosmopolitan center point, offering an extensive variety of diversion choices.

Blloku - The Core of Tirana's Nightlife

Blloku, when a confined region during the socialist time, has changed into the pulsating heart of Tirana's nightlife. This stylish area is fixed with bars, clubs, and cafés, making it the go-to objective for an evening out on the town. A few famous spots in Blloku include:

- **Radio Bar**: A trendy mixed drink bar with a roof patio, ideal for getting a charge out of beverages with a view.

- **Hemingway Bar**: Known for its broad mixed drink menu and energetic climate.

- **Design Club**: A well-known club where you can move the night away to both neighborhood and worldwide DJs.

- **Sky Club**: A housetop club with extraordinary music and an energetic group.

Unrecorded Music and Jazz Bars

Tirana likewise flaunts a flourishing unrecorded music and jazz scene. Settings like Jazz Club and Mullixhiu frequently have live exhibitions including skilled neighborhood artists.

It's an extraordinary method for partaking in a few deep tunes while tasting on your number one beverage.

Late-Night Dining

Albanians love to consolidate their nightlife with late-evening eating. Numerous cafés in Tirana, for example, Oda and Kodra e Diellit, remain open late, serving delightful Albanian and Mediterranean cooking. It's the ideal method for refueling following an evening of moving.

Durres – Beach Clubs and Bars

Durres, a waterfront city along the Adriatic Ocean, offers an exceptional mix of ocean front nightlife and metropolitan diversion. In the mid-year months, Durres turns into a center point for ocean side clubs and outdoors parties.

Beach Clubs

The city's sea shores, for example, Golem Ocean side, change into dynamic party objections around evening time. Ocean side clubs like Summer Club and Dolce Vita have ocean side gatherings, DJ sets, and unrecorded music occasions where you can move under the stars.

Durres Amphitheatre

For a social nightlife experience, look at occasions at the Durres Amphitheatre, a very much protected old Roman amphitheater. It has shows, theater exhibitions, and other far-reaching developments.

Vlora - Seaside Vibes

Vlora, a beautiful seaside town in southern Albania, offers a loose yet pleasant nightlife experience. The city shows signs of life in the late spring months, drawing in the two local people and travelers.

Ocean front Bars

Vlora's ocean front bars, for example, Plazhi Bar and Bora Bora, offer a laid-back air where you can taste mixed drinks and partake in the ocean breeze. These bars frequently have unrecorded music and DJ sets in the nights.

Dusk Views

One of the features of Vlora's nightlife is watching the dusk over the Adriatic Ocean. Go to a beachside bistro, request a beverage, and absorb the stunning perspectives as the sun plunges underneath the skyline.

Saranda - Riviera Nights

Saranda, situated on the Albanian Riviera, is known for its enthusiastic nightlife throughout the mid year season. The town's bars and clubs take special care of a different group, from explorers to upscale voyagers.

Saranda Promenade

The Saranda Promenade wakes up around evening time, with bars and eateries offering a large number of beverages and cooking. It's an extraordinary spot for a comfortable walk and certain individuals watching.

Mango Beach Club

Mango Beach Club is a famous ocean front scene in Saranda known for its gatherings and unrecorded music occasions. It's an optimal spot to move the night away with your feet in the sand.

Beach Parties

Albania's shoreline is spotted with ocean side clubs and outside scenes that host ocean side gatherings throughout the late spring months. These gatherings frequently highlight famous DJs, unrecorded music, and a vivacious climate. Probably the best ocean side party objections in Albania incorporate Ksamil, Jale, and Gjipe Beach.

Themed Gatherings and Festivals

Albania has different themed gatherings and celebrations over time. These occasions take care of various preferences, from electronic dance music (EDM) celebrations to social festivals. Look out for occasions like **Kala Festival**, an electronic live performance set in a beautiful waterfront area.

Security and Enjoyment

While partaking in the nightlife in Albania, it's essential to remain safe and be aware of neighborhood customs. Albanians are known for their warm cordiality, so go ahead and up discussions and make new companions. In any case, as in any objective, playing it safe and watch out for your belongings is fitting.

"Albania Travel Guide 2024" shows that the country's nightlife is a dynamic blend of beach gatherings, metropolitan areas of interest, and social encounters. Whether you're moving under the stars at a beach club in Durres, tasting mixed drinks in the in vogue Blloku neighborhood of Tirana, or getting a charge out of unrecorded music in Saranda, Albania offers a nightlife scene that will leave you with remarkable recollections.

Thus, when the sun goes down, prepare to embrace the energetic and inviting nightlife of this Balkan pearl.

CHAPTER EIGHT
Albania Festivals

Honestly, Albania is a country with a rich embroidery of social practices and celebrations, each offering an extraordinary look into its set of experiences, customs, and energetic soul. Albania's celebration schedule guarantees a different scope of occasions that praise the nation's legacy and present-day impacts. We should leave on an excursion through the dazzling universe of Albanian festivals.

Albania's Festive Tapestry

Albania's celebration schedule is a lively and various embroidery of social, verifiable, and strict festivals. These celebrations give a novel chance to submerge yourself in the rich embroidery of Albanian culture, witness conventional traditions, and experience the glow of Albanian neighborliness.

We should investigate the bright cluster of celebrations that anticipate voyagers in this Balkan jewel.

Tirana International Film Festival (TIFF)

- *When: April*
- *Where: Tirana*

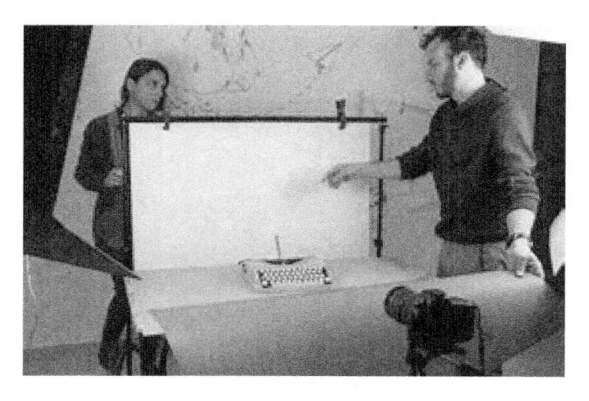

The Tirana World Film Celebration (Spat) is a social diamond that commends the craft of film.

Established in 2003, it has developed to become one of the loftiest film celebrations in the Balkans. Spat grandstands a different determination of global and Albanian movies, including full length motion pictures, narratives, and short movies. It gives a stage to both arising and laid out producers to feature their ability and draw in with crowds.

Dita e Verës (Summer Day)

- *When: Walk fourteenth*

- *Where: From one side of the country to the other*

Dita e Verës, or Summer Day, is a valued Albanian occasion celebrated on Spring fourteenth every year. It denotes the appearance of spring and is a day when individuals eagerly embrace open air exercises, picnics, and celebrations. On this day, you can observer local people wearing customary Albanian dress, taking part in vivacious moving, and partaking in the main indications of the hotter season.

Dita e Flamurit (Flag Day)

- *When: November 28th*

- *Where: Cross country*

Dita e Flamurit, or Flag Day, holds gigantic public importance in Albania. Celebrated on November 28th, this occasion recognizes the day in 1912 when the Albanian flag was first raised, connoting the country's announcement of freedom from the Ottoman Domain. Celebrations incorporate processions, shows, and widespread developments that feature Albanian enthusiasm and pride.

Gjirokastër National Forklore Festival

- *When: July*
- *Where: Gjirokastër*

The Gjirokastër Public Fables Celebration is an energetic festival of Albanian legends and customs. Facilitated in the noteworthy city of Gjirokastër, an UNESCO World Legacy Site known for its very much safeguarded Ottoman design, this celebration unites society music and dance bunches from across Albania and then some. Guests can drench themselves in brilliant exhibitions, respect conventional ensembles, and gain a more profound comprehension of Albania's rich social legacy.

Farkëmijë (Bajram)

- *When: Dates Differ (Islamic Schedule)*

- *Where: Across the country*

Farkëmijë, ordinarily known as Bajram in Albania, is a critical strict occasion celebrated by the country's Muslim people group. It denotes the finish of Ramadan, the Islamic sacred month of fasting. During this merry period, families meet up for unique supplications, elaborate dining experiences, and the trading of gifts. Mosques are delightfully decorated, and roads wake up with the euphoric soul of the occasion.

Rockstock Festival

- *When: August*

- *Where: Dhermi Beach, Albanian Riviera*

Rockstock Celebration is a live performance that happens against the shocking scenery of Dhermi Beach along the Albanian Riviera.

This occasion is a magnet for admirers of exciting music, highlighting a setup of neighborhood and global musical gangs and specialists. Celebration participants can appreciate unrecorded music exhibitions while relaxing in the excellence of the Ionian Ocean, making it a novel and extraordinary melodic experience.

Kala Festival

- *When: June*
- *Where: Dhërmi, Albanian Riviera*

Kala Celebration is an electronic dance music (EDM) celebration that unfurls in the beautiful waterfront town of Dhërmi. It charms electronic music lovers from Albania and all over the planet. The celebration brags an amazing program universally prestigious DJs and specialists who perform in the midst of the stunning scenery of the Albanian Riviera, making an energizing climate of music, dance, and beach front energies.

Festivali I Këngës (Festival of Songs)

- When: December

- Where: Tirana

The Festivali I Këngës, or the Celebration of Melodies, is a yearly music rivalry that has been an essential piece of Albanian culture beginning around 1962. It fills in as the country's public choice cycle for the Eurovision Tune Challenge. The celebration includes a different cluster of melodic classifications, incorporating pop, rock, and customary Albanian music. It finishes in an excellent last occasion, where the victor procures the potential chance to address Albania on the Eurovision stage.

Independent Day

- When: November 28th

- Where: From one side of the country to the other

Indepence Day is a cross country festivity of Albania's statement of freedom from the Ottoman Domain in 1912. Celebrations incorporate processions, shows, and comprehensive developments that grandstand Albania's rich history, nationalism, and solidarity. It's daily when the whole country meets up to consider its excursion to autonomy and the difficulties it has survived.

Virgil Night (Nata e Virgjërë)

- When: Walk 24th

- Where: Across the country

Virgil Night, or Nata e Virgjërë, is a one of a kind Albanian custom celebrated on Spring 24th. It is a night committed to the unbelievable writer Virgil, and individuals accept that on this evening, creatures secure the capacity to talk. It's an evening of narrating, verse recitations, and get-togethers around the chimney. In spite of the fact that it has old agnostic starting points, this custom keeps on being seen in rustic areas of Albania.

Taulantia Festival

- When: July

- Where: Vlorë

The Taulantia Celebration in Vlorë is a festival of old Illyrian legacy and history. It highlights reenactments, customary music, and dance exhibitions that give proper respect to the Illyrian civilization, which once flourished in the area. Guests can investigate authentic shows and find out about the rich tradition of the Illyrians.

Korça Brew Festival

- When: August

- Where: Korça

The Korça Brew Celebration is an energetic occasion that observes Albania's lager culture. Held in the beguiling city of Korça, it unites neighborhood breweries and lager fans. Celebration participants can test different lagers, appreciate unrecorded music, and partake in brew related exercises and games.

Saint Nicholas Day (Dita e Shen Kollit)

- When: December sixth

- Where: From one side of the country to the other

Holy person Nicholas Day, or Dita e Shen Kollit, is an occasion celebrated to pay tribute to Holy person Nicholas, the benefactor holy person of mariners and voyagers. It's daily when anglers and sailors give recognition to the holy person for assurance on their excursions. In beach front towns and towns, you can observer vivid parades, boat gifts, and customary ceremonies.

Summer Festival on the Albanian Riviera

The Albanian Riviera wakes up with summer festivals during the hotter months. These celebrations frequently include unrecorded music, craftsmanship shows, social exhibitions, and various outside exercises. Whether you're in Saranda, Himara, or Dhërmi, you're probably going to coincidentally find a celebration that adds an additional layer of fervor to your beach front escape.

Religious Celebrations

Albania is a country with a rich strict legacy, and different strict celebrations and festivities are noticed over time. These incorporate Christian, Muslim, and Bektashi celebrations, each offering a remarkable knowledge into the country's different strict practices.

Local and Regional Festivals

Notwithstanding these significant celebrations, Albania brags a plenty neighborhood and provincial festivals. These frequently base on unambiguous towns, areas, or widespread developments. They are a brilliant method for encountering the true and various social embroidery of Albania.

Culinary Festivals

Albanian cooking is commended with fervor at culinary celebrations that feature the country's conventional dishes and culinary advancements.

From baklava to byrek, these celebrations are a dining experience for the faculties.

"Albania Travel Guide 2024" unveils a dazzling excursion through the country's rich history, culture, and customs. Whether you're going to the Spat in Tirana, moving the night away at Kala Celebration, or relishing the kinds of Albanian cooking at a culinary celebration, you'll be drenched in the country's lively soul aSSnd inviting cordiality. As you plan your movements in Albania, ensure to check the celebration schedule to add a hint of merriment to your experience in this Balkan diamond.

CHAPTER NINE
Safety Tips for Travelling to Albania

Guaranteeing your wellbeing while at the same time voyaging is vital, and Albania is no exemption. As you leave on your excursion to investigate the rich social legacy, staggering scenes, and warm neighborliness of Albania in 2024, it's vital for be good to go and informed about wellbeing measures. This far reaching guide will give you important wellbeing tips and bits of knowledge to make your visit to Albania a smooth and secure insight.

Exploring Albania Safely

Going to Albania in 2024 vows to be a fulfilling and enhancing experience, yet like any objective, focusing on wellbeing all through your journey is fundamental. Albania has taken critical steps in working on its security and framework as of late, making it an undeniably famous objective for voyagers. Notwithstanding, it's as yet insightful to remain informed and play it safe to guarantee a protected and pleasant excursion. Here are far reaching wellbeing ways to go in Albania:

Research and Planning

Before you even set foot in Albania, exhaustive examination and arranging are vital to a protected excursion. Here are things to consider:

- **Check Travel Advisories**: Preceding your excursion, counsel your administration's tourism warning site to remain refreshed on any wellbeing related data or cautions for Albania.

- **Visa and Entry Requirements**: Guarantee you have the essential visas and documentation to enter Albania, and check the lapse date of your identification.

- **Travel Insurance**: Buy far reaching travel protection that covers health related crises, trip abrogations, and individual effects. Check assuming that your approach incorporates inclusion for exercises you intend to participate in.

- **Itinerary and Accommodations**: Offer your movement agenda with a confided in companion or relative. Book facilities ahead of time, particularly in the event that you're going during the pinnacle vacationer season.

Health and Medical Preparations

Dealing with your wellbeing while at the same time voyaging is essential. This is the way to plan:

- *Vaccinations*: Counsel your medical care supplier or a movement center about suggested immunizations for Albania. Hepatitis An and B, typhoid, and lockjaw are normally encouraged.

- *Doctor prescribed Medications*: Assuming that you require physician endorsed meds, guarantee you have a satisfactory stock for your outing and convey them in their unique compartments with clear names. Conveying a duplicate of your prescriptions is likewise shrewd.

- *Travel Health Kit*: Pack a movement wellbeing unit that incorporates fundamental emergency treatment supplies, non-prescription drugs, bug repellent, sunscreen, and any private clinical supplies you might require.

- *Medical Facilities*: Find out about the area of clinical offices and emergency clinics in the areas you intend to visit. The bigger urban communities, like Tirana and Vlora, have exceptional emergency clinics.

Safety on the Road

Albania's scenes are best investigated by street, yet it's essential to be mindful while driving or utilizing public transportation:

- *Driving*: Assuming you intend to drive in Albania, know that street conditions can fluctuate. Practice alert, submit to traffic rules, and drive protectively. Safety belts are required for all travelers.

- *Public Transportation*: Utilize legitimate transportation suppliers, particularly for really long travel. Be wary while utilizing taxis, and choose authorized taxis with meters. In Tirana, ride-sharing applications like Uber and Bolt are accessible.

- *Road Signage*: Find out about Albanian street signs and traffic guidelines. Streets can be tight and twisting in certain areas, so drive cautiously.

Personal Safety

While Albania is for the most part thought to be protected, playing it safe is savvy:

- *Remain Alert*: Focus on your environmental factors, particularly in packed regions and places of interest. Be wary of pickpockets in occupied places like business sectors and public transportation.

- *Stay away from Ostentatious Displays*: It's ideal to keep costly gems, hardware, and assets hid to try not to draw pointless consideration.

-Respect Local Customs: Albania is a socially different country with its practices and customs. Recognize neighborhood culture, including clothing regulations for strict destinations.

- *Emergency Numbers*: Remember or have simple admittance to crisis numbers. In Albania, the widespread crisis number is 112 for police, clinical, and fire crises.

Natural Disasters and Outdoor Safety

Albania's normal excellence is one of its features, however it's crucial for stay protected while investigating open air attractions:

- *Weather*: Actually take a look at weather conditions conjectures prior to setting out on open air exercises. Albania can encounter weighty downpour and periodic floods, particularly in rugged regions.

- *Hiking and Adventure Activities* In the event that you intend to climb or participate in experience sports, consider recruiting a neighborhood guide who knows the landscape and can guarantee your wellbeing.

- *Wildlife*: Albania is home to different natural life, remembering bears and wolves for distant regions. Instruct yourself about the neighborhood natural life and avoid potential risk while setting up camp or climbing.

Local Laws and Regulations

Regarding nearby regulations and guidelines is pivotal for a difficulty free outing:

- *Drug Laws*: Ownership or utilization of unlawful medications is totally precluded and can bring about extreme punishments.

- *Photography*: Consistently request consent prior to taking photographs of individuals, particularly in country regions. A few local people might be awkward with photography.

- *Littering*: Discard rubbish capably and regard the climate. Littering is likely to fines.

- *Social Sites*: While visiting social or strict destinations, dress humbly and observe a particular guidelines or rules gave.

Language and Communication

While numerous Albanians in vacationer regions communicate in English, knowing a few fundamental Albanian expressions for communication is useful. Conveying an interpretation application or a phrasebook can be gainful in far off regions where English may not be generally spoken.

Currency and Finances

Albania utilizes the Albanian Lek (ALL) as its money. It's fitting to convey a blend of money and credit/charge cards. ATMs are generally accessible in significant urban communities, yet they might be more uncommon in provincial regions.

Local Cuisine and Water Safety

Getting a charge out of Albanian food is a feature of any excursion, yet all at once be mindful:

- *Food Safety*: Eat at trustworthy cafés and road sellers with great cleanliness rehearses. Try not to devour crude or half-cooked fish.

- *Water Safety*: It's fitting to hydrate and keep away from regular water except if it's unequivocally named as safe for drinking.

Cultural Sensitivity

Albania is a different country with a blend of strict convictions and social practices. Recognize neighborhood customs, customs, and strict locales.

Travel Insurance and Documentation

Keep duplicates of fundamental travel archives, including your identification, visa, travel protection, and flight agenda. Store these independently from the firsts in the event of misfortune or robbery.

Local Advice

If all else fails, look for exhortation from local people or individual voyagers. They can give important bits of knowledge and proposals to safe travel in Albania.

Emergency Contacts

- *Police: 112*
- *Medical Emergency: 112*
- *Fire Department: 112*
- *Tourist Police: +355 4 2233 602*

By following these exhaustive wellbeing tips, you can partake in a solid and noteworthy excursion through Albania in 2024. Embrace the country's rich culture, staggering scenes, and warm friendliness while guaranteeing your prosperity all through your experience in this Balkan diamond. Safe voyages!

CONCLUSION

As we draw this extensive "Albania Travel Guide 2024" to a close, you're now armed with a wealth of knowledge and insights to embark on a memorable journey through Albania in 2024. This Balkan gem, with its rich cultural heritage, stunning landscapes, and warm hospitality, beckons travelers from around the world. Throughout this guide, we've covered a range of topics, from the breathtaking landscapes and cultural attractions to the practical aspects of planning your trip and ensuring your safety. Let's bring it all together in this comprehensive conclusion.

Albania, frequently alluded to as "Europe's Last Secret," is a country that has remained largely unseen by mass the travel industry, making it an unlikely treasure for valiant explorers. Settled in the core of the Balkans, Albania offers an enrapturing mix of regular excellence, rich history, and warm cordiality.

Albania's scene is an embroidery of normal marvels ready to be investigated. From the immaculate sea shores of the Albanian Riviera to the rough pinnacles of the Damned Mountains, this nation offers a different scope of outside encounters. Whether you're an experience devotee looking for adrenaline-siphoning exercises or a nature sweetheart longing for peaceful minutes, Albania has everything.

The social legacy of Albania is a demonstration of its novel history and the impacts of different civic establishments. Investigate old vestiges like Butrint, an UNESCO World Legacy Site, and dig into the middle age appeal of towns like Gjirokastër and Berat. Albania's rich embroidery of customs and customs is best capable through its celebrations, which celebrate all that from film and music to old stories and strict observances.

Before you set out on your Albanian experience, cautious arranging is fundamental to guarantee a consistent and pleasant excursion.

Understanding Albania's topography and street network is pivotal for an effective excursion. Outfitted with a decent guide and GPS, you can explore the country's different landscape, from rugged districts to waterfront towns. Focus on street signs and be ready for winding streets and shifting street conditions, particularly in country regions.

A very much arranged trip is the groundwork of a noteworthy excursion. Guarantee you have the important visas and documentation to enter Albania, and check the termination date of your identification. Book facilities ahead of time, particularly on the off chance that you're going during the pinnacle vacationer season. Travel protection is an unquestionable requirement, covering health related crises, trip retractions, and individual effects.

In the event that you're considering how to capitalize on your time in Albania, our seven-day schedule plan gives a reasonable blend of social investigation, outside undertakings, and unwinding. Beginning in the capital, Tirana, you'll travel through Albania's features, from old destinations to immaculate sea shores, enchanting towns to rough mountains.

Albania brags an abundance must-visit attractions that exhibit its set of experiences, culture, and regular magnificence. Investigate the old remnants of Apollonia, climb through Valbona Public Park, and appreciate the appeal of seaside jewels like Saranda and Himara. These top attractions offer a brief look into the essence of Albania.

Albania's shore along the Ionian and Adriatic Oceans is a gold mine of dazzling sea shores. From the popular Ksamil Ocean side to stowed away bays along the Albanian Riviera, you'll track down a piece of heaven for sun-searchers and ocean side sweethearts. Jump into the perfectly clear waters, loosen up on the sandy shores, and relish new fish at beachside tavernas.

No excursion to Albania is finished without enjoying its luscious food. From flavorful byrek to delicious barbecued meats, Albanian food is a culinary excursion in itself. Investigate neighborhood markets, eat at conventional cafés, and appreciate the kinds of this unexpected, yet invaluable treasure of Balkan cooking.

Albania's nightlife scene is lively and fiery, with something for each taste. From clamoring clubs in Tirana to beachside bars in the Albanian Riviera, you can move the night away or loosen up with a mixed drink while taking in the picturesque perspectives. Albania's nightlife mirrors the country's energetic energy and vitality.

Similarly as with any movement objective, it is fundamental to guarantee your security. While Albania is for the most part thought to be ok for travelers, it's fundamental for play it safe to guarantee a solid and pleasant outing.

Exhaustive examination and arranging are your initial moves toward a protected excursion. Actually look at tourism warnings, guarantee your documentation is all together, and put resources into complete travel protection. Share your schedule with a confided in companion or relative, and get to know crisis contact numbers.

Your wellbeing ought to be a main concern while voyaging. Counsel your medical care supplier for suggested immunizations, convey physician recommended prescriptions in their unique compartments, and pack a movement wellbeing unit. Know about the area of clinical offices in the areas you intend to visit.

Whether you're driving or utilizing public transportation, practice alert out and about. Know about nearby traffic guidelines, utilize legitimate transportation suppliers, and lock in while driving. Remain watchful, particularly in jam-packed regions and places of interest.

Remain caution to your environmental factors, keep away from gaudy presentations of riches, and regard neighborhood customs and customs. Watch out for your possessions, particularly in jam-packed puts, and be mindful while utilizing ATMs or taxicabs. Find out about neighborhood regulations and guidelines to stay away from any lawful issues.

While investigating Albania's regular magnificence, watch out for the climate, particularly in rocky districts inclined to weighty downpour and floods. In the event that you intend to take part in open air exercises, consider recruiting a neighborhood guide who knows the territory. Be mindful of untamed life in far off regions and practice dependable setting up camp and climbing.

Learning a few fundamental Albanian expressions can upgrade your movement experience and work with correspondence. Convey interpretation applications or phrasebooks for regions where English may not be generally spoken.

Grasping the neighborhood money, utilizing a blend of money and cards, and approaching ATMs in significant urban communities can assist you with dealing with your funds flawlessly during your outing.

Getting a charge out of Albanian cooking is a feature of your excursion, however be careful about where and what you eat. Pick legitimate cafés and road merchants, and try not to eat crude or half-cooked fish. Hydrate to guarantee your security.

Albania is a socially different country with a blend of strict convictions and practices. Recognize neighborhood customs, dress humbly while visiting social or strict locales, and consistently request authorization prior to taking photographs of individuals, particularly in country regions.

Keep duplicates of fundamental travel records and store them independently from the firsts. Guarantee your movement protection inclusion is modern and incorporates the exercises you intend to take part in.

If all else fails, look for exhortation from local people or individual explorers who can give significant experiences and suggestions.

Retain or have simple admittance to crisis contact numbers, including the general crisis number 112 for police, clinical, and fire crises.

Albania, with its enamoring scenes, rich culture, and warm neighborliness, is an objective that guarantees a genuinely one of a kind travel insight. As you leave on your excursion through this unlikely treasure in the core of the Balkans, recollect that cautious preparation and wellbeing precautionary measures are your partners in guaranteeing a consistent and secure experience.

From the clamoring roads of Tirana to the serene shores of the Albanian Riviera, from old remains saturated with history to dynamic celebrations praising practice and innovation, Albania is a nation ready to be found. Whether you're an open air devotee looking for exciting undertakings or a social traveler digging into the past, Albania offers a different cluster of encounters that will make a permanent imprint on your movements.

As you embrace Albania's secret fortunes, relish its culinary enjoyments, and drench yourself in its celebrations, consistently keep security at the very front of your excursion. By following the security tips illustrated in this aide, you'll safeguard yourself as well as upgrade your capacity to enjoy each experience of this charming journey.

"Albania Travel Guide 2024" is an encouragement to investigate, to associate with local people who will greet you wholeheartedly, and to make enduring recollections. In this way, gather your sacks, set up your schedule, and set out on an extraordinary experience through Albania — a place that is known for variety, magnificence, and perpetual revelation. Safe ventures, and may your Albanian process be loaded up with amazement and wonderment.

Printed in Great Britain
by Amazon